# ARTIFICIAL IN

What Everyone Needs to Know Today About Our Future

# ARTIFICIAL INTELLIGENCE

What Everyone Needs to Know Today About Our Future

# CONTENTS

# INTRODUCTION

I want to thank you and congratulate you for buying the book, *"Artificial Intelligence"*

This book contains proven steps and strategies on how to accomplish things better with the help of artificial intelligence.

With the introduction of artificial intelligence in our society, life has become more diverse, fast-paced, and more convenient. Since the birth of AI research back in 1956 at Dartmouth College, creative minds have strived to create machines dramatically that are as intelligent as humans are. These human machines designed by humans, for humans, and to think like humans will help us do things better, faster, and more cost-efficient.

Most people think that artificial intelligence will substitute manual labor and decrease job opportunities. In fact, the opposite is true. In this book, you will learn how artificial intelligence provides more job opportunities.

Automation does not mean that machines will replace humans.

You will also learn how artificial intelligence benefits industries such as transportation, tourism, healthcare, education, retail and agriculture, banking and finance, sales and marketing.

This book covers fascinating facts about artificial intelligence that you may have encountered or have yet to see. You will learn about robots that help in households, chatbots, self-driving cars and robo-taxis, and even those in healthcare. Artificial intelligence promises excellent opportunities for business processes, the job market, and healthcare.

If you think that you can live without artificial intelligence, think again. AI is very much part of our everyday lives. From smartphones that remind you of meetings to apps that count how many steps you've taken. AI is already embedded in our lives and continue to do so.

Thanks again for buying this book, I hope you enjoy it!

# CHAPTER 1

## UNDERSTANDING ARTIFICIAL INTELLIGENCE

"Some people call this artificial intelligence, but the reality is this technology will enhance us. So instead of artificial intelligence, I think we'll augment our intelligence." – Ginni Rometty

When talking about the promises or perils that artificial intelligence may offer us, it is essential to understand what it is exactly. Technically speaking, artificial intelligence is the component of science that aims to create intelligent machines that function like humans. Engineers, computer scientists, and technical specialists strive to develop machines that act and react like humans. Among the activities that the technology brings are planning, learning, speech recognition, and problem-solving.

However, research highlights some of the challenges in programming computers for artificial intelligence. These issues include reasoning, knowledge, perception, learning, strategic planning, problem-solving, and the ability to manipulate objects. The only way that machines can function very much like humans is when there is an abundant source of information from the outside world. This poses a significant challenge because machines cannot replicate reasoning, perception, and common sense, which are associated with brain faculties.

## A Short History

Artificial intelligence officially started in the 1940s with the introduction of the programmable digital computer. It focused more on mathematical reasoning. With this innovation, scientists were inspired to come up with an electronic brain.

With the foundation of AI research in 1956 at Dartmouth College, funding for research and development poured in. However, in 1973, the US and the British governments decided to halt funding due to the difficulties brought about by hardware limitations. Seven years after, the Japanese government inspired others to fund billions of dollars to continue the research but stopped again during the late 1980s. By the turn of the 21st century, machine learning permeated educational institutions and industries.

## Components of Artificial Intelligence

For artificial intelligence to be successful, there are some requirements that it needs to meet.

First is discovery. An intelligent system must learn techniques such as reduction, segmentation, and risk detection. This must be done with minimal human intervention. An intelligent system should be able to discover the techniques based on a set of data. Asking the proper questions to obtain data is also crucial.

The second component is prediction. Given the set of data, an intelligent system should be able to predict what lies in the future. It must classify, regress, and rank accordingly. The system should also determine which data are risky.

The third one is justification. Applications should be able to justify its features and support human interaction. For example, cars have alarm systems that alert drivers when something is wrong. An intelligent system should also have the ability to repair itself when the need arises.

The fourth component is action. Intelligent systems need to execute actions according to discovery, prediction, and justification.

Learning is the fifth component. An intelligent application should have the ability to learn continuously and improve itself.

The above components may seem far-fetched. The human brain is a complex organ that is very difficult to replicate. Human brains have cells that form a network of communication. Another aspect of the human brain is emotions. It is impossible to teach a machine emotions and feelings because it is not a living thing.

Even though it seems impossible, data scientists and engineers continue to find ways to create intelligent systems that will make people's lives better. In fact, many institutions have completed many projects.

In 2017, NASA discovered two new planets with machine learning. They used existing data from the Kepler telescope and discovered the new planets. Due to artificial intelligence, NASA has found a new planetary system towards new knowledge.

Another innovation is the Leka Smart Toy, which supports children with developmental disorders in interacting with others. The toy aims to facilitate learning by developing interpersonal skills.

Artificial intelligence poses problems as well as promises. It has been more than a century since great minds have come up with this innovative idea. To date, more and more innovations are implemented due to the success of data scientists, computer experts, and engineers. In the next chapters, you will learn about how artificial intelligence continuously improves our lives.

# CHAPTER 2

## **ARTIFICIAL INTELLIGENCE AT WORK**

Artificial intelligence is now transforming our economy through machine learning. Computers and machines learn from experience and imitate humans in making decisions. Artificial intelligence benefits different industries by taking care of routine tasks, analyzing customer behavior through data, reducing operational costs, and many more.

Let's have a look at how artificial intelligence is shaping the economy.

## Banking and Finance

PayPal is one of the classic examples of how artificial intelligence works in handling transactions. The system analyzes transactions and prevents fraud.

Another example is JPMorgan Chase's Contract Intelligence (COiN) platform. The system analyzes legal documents then extracts important clauses and data points. Numerous agreements can now be reviewed in a matter of a few seconds.

Wells Fargo piloted a chatbot via Facebook Messenger that provides account information and helps users reset their passwords.

On the other hand, Bank of America also has its virtual assistant named Erica. This chatbot uses "predictive analysis and cognitive messaging" and offers financial guidance to millions of customers.

Another classic example of artificial intelligence in the banking industry is the mobile banking application. Customers can now perform transactions without visiting the banks. Sending and receiving money, paying bills, purchasing goods and services, and investing are much easier with mobile apps.

Most large banks have started using mobile check deposits. No need for a bank client to visit a bank physically just to deposit a check. Mitek, which uses machine learning and AI, deciphers and converts handwriting through optical character recognition (OCR).

Credit decisions are also easier. Consumers no longer have to wait for a week or more just to determine their credit standing. FICO uses machine learning and puts together data, which determines an individual's credit score. This poses less risk and reduces the financial institution's losses due to delinquent customers.

## Healthcare

Artificial intelligence is evident in healthcare such as X-ray machines, CT scans, ultrasound, and numerous other tests. The machines analyze the patient's data that are essential for treatment plans.

An example that uses machine learning is Microsoft's Hanover Project. With natural language processing, it predicts the most effective drug treatment for individual cancer patients.

Molly by Sense.ly is a virtual nurse that hears the patient out and offers clinical advice and services.

The Babylon AI doctor app, through speech recognition, listens to patients, discovers their symptoms, and suggests possible treatments.

Nuance Communications recently launched an artificial virtual assistant that aims to help avoid doctor burnout. The application uses speech recognition and discusses lab results and possible treatments based on a given set of data. The application also aims to increase the interaction between doctor and patient by focusing on crucial aspects of the consultation.

Baidu, which is China's version of Google, developed DuLight, which is a device for the visually impaired. The device is attached to the ear, scans surrounding objects, and describes objects according to how a person experiences them in reality. Baidu's DuLight is successful in providing the "vision" and helps visually impaired people function well in life.

## Retail and Manufacturing

Amazon, an e-commerce platform, uses recommender systems and is an example of artificial intelligence in e-commerce. It uses machine learning and predictive analysis to recommend items for each customer.

Chatbots and virtual customer assistants are also on every e-commerce website. They answer customers' queries, make suggestions, or direct them to a specific website, department, or contact person.

In manufacturing companies, robots or machines have replaced humans in performing dangerous jobs such as carrying large equipment, handling and disposing of chemicals, cutting raw materials, and sorting into packages. These provide more safety and decreases burnout for the workers.

## Technology

The best examples of artificial intelligence are Apple's Siri, Microsoft's Cortana, Google Assistant, and Amazon's Alexa. The applications use speech recognition, predictive analysis, and user data to respond to your orders. Although users may encounter challenges with third-party applications, they seem to work well. For example, you could ask Siri to read your email, send a text, or book an Uber. You could also ask Google Assistant for directions to the Empire State Building and find out how the traffic is. You'd have to test the applications though and see which one suits you best, based on your needs.

Google also has smart email categorization. Gmail can categorize your mail according to social mail, promotional mail, primary mail, and priority mail. When you mark a specific email as "important," Google's algorithm "remembers" it and delivers future emails to your priority inbox. Google even introduced the "smart reply" feature that recommends replies based on the email that you received.

On the other hand, Skype and Google Translate offer translation services in real-time. You can receive a message in a different language and have it translated.

Facebook uses face recognition is another excellent example of AI. It recognizes people from your photos and recommends that you tag them. It also recognizes your current location and provides places that you can go to.

AI and machine learning also help cybersecurity by analyzing user behavior and detecting expected actions rather than detecting outdated or unknown digital signatures. It creates more security and identifies potential risks right away. An example of this is Aetna's new behavior-based security system that monitors the users' devices and applies biometric protection rather than requiring passwords.

## Education

In higher education, personalized learning is made available through artificial intelligence. Data analytics collect and analyze data based on student performance. It allows educators to tailor the learning materials according to students' needs.

One example is the automated text analysis program of the University of Michigan. It analyses writing material, identifies the strengths as well as the weaknesses, and makes recommendations for improvement.

Tutoring software, such as Carnegie Learning's Mika software, uses cognitive science to provide customized tutoring and real-time feedback based on student's needs. This software targets remedial students.

Virtual facilitators are also available to those who opt to study at home. Students can now enroll online and attend classes in the comforts of their own home. This opportunity makes it easier for working students, single parents, and those with physical disabilities to continue learning.

## Energy and Utilities

One example where AI is used in energy and utilities are apps that monitor consumption. Users can input the electrical appliance, time used, and average monthly consumption and get an estimate of the usage costs. This helps users manage their electricity consumption and bills.

With the introduction of smart grids, energy companies can predict power surges, fluctuations, and weak spots. Energy companies can easily respond to these issues and inform consumers. Being able to observe equipment and analyze the data will help energy companies detect failures and avoid mishaps.

In Canada and in 19 US states, wind power generators are controlled by machine learning. SpaceTime developed a software that boosts wind turbine functions, creates ideal schedules, and routine maintenance for better performance and diagnostics. This leads to a reduction of maintenance costs and efficiency.

## Transportation and Automotive

At present, the best example of artificial intelligence in the automotive industry is the presence of self-driving cars.

Tesla pioneered autonomous cars, which helped prevent vehicular accidents through a number of safety systems. It alerts the driver when his hands are off the wheel, when beyond the speed limit, at crossroads, proximity to obstructions, or even humans and animals that are not clearly visible. The autopilot function stops the car when faced with these obstructions.

Ride-sharing services, such as Uber, is another example of artificial intelligence. Owning a car is not a privilege anymore because you can easily hail a private car to pick you up and drop you off using an application. Security and safety are not compromised because you will have details such as the driver's name, vehicle identification number, make and model of the car. You can even send your route to your family members, and they can track your journey real-time.

Commercial airplanes have been using AI technology since 1914. Airplanes run on autopilot most of the time. Human Intervention is needed only during take-off and landing.

Google Analytics also uses data from Google maps and the traffic app Waze to analyze routes and reduce commute times. Since Waze encourages users to share their location, traffic condition, and other information such as accidents or blockades, more data is fed into the app. More data equates to better algorithms.

As you can see, artificial intelligence is clearly present nowadays. Without these innovations, certain services will have limited availability for senior citizens, handicapped people, and those with medical conditions.

Artificial intelligence continues to make our lives better. In the next chapters, you will learn more about the benefits of artificial intelligence.

# CHAPTER 3

## BENEFITS OF ARTIFICIAL INTELLIGENCE

"Everything we love about civilization is a product of intelligence, so amplifying our human intelligence with artificial intelligence has the potential of helping civilization flourish like never before – as long as we manage to keep the technology beneficial." – Max Tegmark

If you've heard of or watched the movie "A.I. Artificial Intelligence" played by Haley Joel Osment, you' wonder if it could possibly come true in the future. In the movie, David (played by Osmont) is the first programmed robotic boy that is taught emotions. He becomes the son of his inventor and embarks on a journey of self-discovery. In the movie, you'll find that it is good to have a son for a robot, especially for parents who've had trouble conceiving.

Max Tegmark, the president of the Future of Life Insitute, made a good point when he said that we must keep technology beneficial. Humans are still in control of artificial intelligence no matter how smart they get. Humans have the power to make lives better with the aid of artificial intelligence.

Despite the misgivings about artificial intelligence, let's explore the many reasons that AI benefits people and economies.

## Enhanced Efficiency

Humans no longer have to deal with tedious and monotonous tasks. Leave the manual work to machines and focus on building relationships and interpersonal connections. In factories, production is faster, efficient and error-free. Workers can avoid accidents because they do not need to take on dangerous tasks. Falling asleep on a tedious job is farfetched because humans become more productive and leave the boring jobs to machines.

## More Jobs, Better Economy

Contrary to popular belief, AI will not destroy jobs. In fact, there will be more job opportunities open wherein humans can work better with the aid of machines. New jobs will be available to the workforce because machine learning needs to be managed by people who are adept at the job. For example, in the past switchboard operators need to plug in phone plugs manually and participate in the call. Nowadays, computers run switchboards. Switchboard operators can move on to better jobs in customer service, as secretaries, or receptionists, which have better human interaction.

Did you know that lifts or elevators were controlled manually in the past? An operator controlled a very large lever and had to estimate and judge when the lift stops. Now, you can simply push a button and get to the desired floor.

In China, 90% of manual labor has been replaced by robots, which resulted in better quality, fewer defects, and increased production. This means that the laborers can now move on to better jobs such as maintenance and quality control.

Higher productivity leads to a stronger economy. Humans will have more time for family, establishing connections, interpersonal relationships, and better work communication.

## Lifestyle Enhancements

With artificial intelligence, virtual assistants can respond to emails and perform data entry work more efficiently. Homeowners can have access to innovations that help reduce energy consumption and improve home security through alarm systems. Enhancements to healthcare are also made possible as proven by better diagnoses. Doctors can focus on communicating with the patients, which improves doctor-patient relationship.

## Better Business

Since most mundane tasks have become automated, business operational costs are reduced. Businesses can focus on furthering client relationships and improve products and services than dealing with attrition due to boredom, work hazards due to machines, and maintain old machines. Furthermore, the error is greatly reduced due to the specific data fed to the machines that are applied strictly to the tasks. For example, calculating numerous data will be error-free, thus reducing the risk of inaccurate computations and incorrect business decisions.

## Enhances Creativity

Humans are becoming more creative at coming up with innovations using artificial intelligence. For example, early Facebook users have noticed that the Social Network now suggests helpful articles based on your posts and searches. These algorithms make Facebook more engaging and motivate you to use the platform. Researchers are also becoming more creative in coming up with solutions to everyday problems.

# CHAPTER 4

## HOW AI CHANGES OUR LIVES

Some people may find it unnerving that computers are becoming smarter than people. Yet, you have to admit that artificial intelligence makes things easier.

One example is Google Drive photos. Google "recognizes" faces, places, and images that when you type "beach" it shows you photos you've taken on a beach. This is very helpful when you're looking for that very old birthday photo you took yet you don't remember when.

Your email's spam filter automatically sends spam mail to the junk mailbox by analyzing how you categorize your email. Amazon and Spotify algorithms recommend music, books, and products based on your preferences, searches, and browsing history. Google maps and other mobile map software suggest routes based on traffic conditions and your travel patterns. Speech recognition software such as Siri or Google Assistant not only recognizes your words but the tone of your voice. You can even speak in one language, and is automatically translated to the language of whomever you're talking to.

The above examples demonstrate how artificial intelligence has become a part of our lives. You have to admit that they make our days easier by taking care of the trivial matters.

Skeptics and other experts argue that artificial intelligence may cause risks as well.

There are always two sides to a coin, and artificial intelligence is not spared. One of the top concerns is that a superintelligence may be created that can banish all of humanity.

Another posing danger is that since AI is programmed to do something, it will ignore all other circumstances just to achieve its goal. A good example is heat-seeking missiles. It will seek its target no matter what it is and may not distinguish between an enemy warship and a burning house that has been hit by the enemy.

If these programmed machines fall into the wrong hands, they may be used for an intent that is not aligned with what it was created for. For example, a superhuman robot that was created to carry heavy loads may be used to haul tons of illegal shipment without being monitored by police.

Given the challenges, data scientists and engineers still aim to create artificial intelligence machines for the betterment of society. It is only a matter of who controls them. That is why the government and other private institutions are also careful in funding research. The goals of the project are analyzed well before being granted.

## Importance of Artificial Intelligence

You cannot deny that artificial intelligence forms a crucial part of advanced technology. Artificial intelligence helps people cope with advancements in this fast-paced world.

AI is important not only because it performs automated tasks, but it also performs the tasks, frequently, delivers high-volume, with reliability, and without getting tired. Human interaction is still needed to ensure that the machine still performs according to requirements.

AI also upgrades existing products. Chatbots and smart machines are made more interactive rather than robotic. Large amounts of data fed into AI machines are also analyzed to make the product better.

Progressive learning algorithms help AI adapt, analyze data, and program itself. Through AI, algorithms acquire new skills. AI can also analyze more data and develop a fraud system. The more data it receives, the more efficiently they perform due to accuracy. Therefore, deep learning is made possible through speech recognition, object recognition, image classification.

Furthermore, self-learning algorithms cause healthy competition. Those with the best data comes out at the top. Therefore, it encourages creative minds to come up with more innovative and unique solutions.

# CHAPTER 5

## AI AND SAVING LIVES

When talking about saving lives, it does not only focus on healthcare. Many innovations were designed to save lives or promote better health.

First, artificial intelligence is evident in healthcare. X-ray machines, ultrasound devices, and CT scans provide customized readings to help diagnose your sickness and provide treatments. Virtual healthcare assistants communicate with the patients and remind them to take their medication, follow-up on a doctor's appointment, eat healthily and exercise regularly. They can even become health coaches.

Cancer treatments have become better thanks to artificial intelligence. AI scours through numerous data of previous cancer situations, analyzes them, compares them with an existing patient's condition, and makes specific recommendations. Therefore, the doctor can then provide specific medication based on the specific type of cancer that an individual has. The best example is the AI software Watson, which was piloted at the University of Tokyo's Institute of Medical Science. A 60-year-old woman had a rare type of leukemia, and the first anti-cancer treatments did not work. When they used Watson, in 10 minutes, they were able to find out the exact type of leukemia and treat her with the correct drugs that saved her life. With the help of Watson, they were able to compare her genetic data with numerous cancer studies and identify the exact type of cancer.

During surgeries, doctors can "watch" through a widescreen and observe the operation as it goes. Consulting doctors can make recommendations based on what they see even when they are outside the operating room. This leads to more elbow room for those in the actual operation and less exposure to infection for the patients.

Second, security home alarms, on the other hand, are programmed to detect unusual movement outside your home and send you a warning should there be an intruder. You can also program it to send a distress signal to the doctor, police station, or fire station as needed.

Autonomous cars, such as Tesla and BMW, make driving safer for the driver, passengers, and other motorists. It monitors the driver's body signals and can detect if the driver is sleepy or intoxicated based on movement and body temperature. It alerts the driver through deafening sounds when the car is driving erratically or when the driver's hands are not on the wheel. It stops when it detects obstructions such as oncoming traffic, crossways, obstacles, humans, or animals that were not visible to the driver. Autonomous cars can even park for you.

Suicide-related deaths have also been one of the things that AI is trying to solve. For example, the AI Buddy Project, which uses animated characters, act as an interactive buddy for children whose parents are at war or who have lost them at war. AI can not replace emotional connections, but families were able to detect suicidal tendencies and prevented them. Brain scans were also used in psychological research and psychiatric treatments to detect suicidal tendencies of patients with mental health problems.

On the other hand, Bark.us used machine learning to analyze communications via email, social media platforms, and text messages to scan for language that may be related to suicidal tendencies. The software alerts family members or guardians should it detect these tendencies in an individual.

Additionally, defense systems also utilize artificial intelligence. Intelligent systems replace soldiers in monitoring and groundwork, which saves the soldiers' lives, the community's lives, and benefits the army. For example, a bomb disposal robot can strategically place the bombs without accidentally defusing it. Soldiers don't have to go into the battlefield and risk their lives just to plant bombs. Also, some robots are aimed precisely at targets. Due to the accuracy, it only aims at the intended targets and won't miss, which prevents the loss of innocent lives. Robots also help in clearing a site of booby trips. Military intelligence units often disguise bombs or traps as everyday objects such as stones, bottles, or cigarette packs. Robots have sensors that can detect wirings and systems associated with booby traps. This is also the same technology used in airports to detect bombs or explosives.

Now you see that, artificial intelligence does more than just make lives easier. It even extends lives, preserves lives, and saves lives.

# CHAPTER 6

## WHAT THE FUTURE LOOKS LIKE

Now that you have learned about how artificial intelligence is already part of our lives let's explore the future. This is just the tip of the iceberg. There are numerous possibilities out there, and more institutions are developing AI research.

First, transportation looks promising. At present, you can't help but be amazed at how smart cars lead to safer driving and fewer accidents. Uber is now on the verge of launching robo-taxis. With this project, the shift will be to consume car services rather than own one. As a result, it will be more cost-effective and convenient. The car's design will also dramatically change due to functionality. Instead of the constraining steering wheel, control panels replace it. Seats may also be rearranged for more passenger room. With the introduction of self-driving cars, robo-taxis, and ride-sharing the number of vehicles on the road will significantly reduce.

Second, smart offices will build better working relationships and encourage productivity. Imagine having the ability to "teleport" from one office to another when you need to attend a meeting or conference, you can do this in the future with the help of virtual reality. Vuzix is already on its toes developing "smart glasses" that provide information based on analytics. People can even meet "virtually" in 3D via a simulated office. AI may also analyze your routines and tasks and seat you with people whom you can collaborate with. No need to purchase desks that are unused because employees don't use them.

Third, in education, researchers are also coming up with innovations that make education convenient and a global experience. For example, virtual facilitators can be made available to students who have challenges in commuting. 3D gaming, computer animation, and simulations pave the way for interactive learning. Another example is USC Institute's "Captivating Virtual Instruction for Training" which delivers an engaging and stimulating course material for participants. Machine learning also looks promising in identifying at-risk students and decreasing the dropout rates by providing alternative learning.

Fourth, in banking and finance, Wealthfront announced that it was plunging into the AI revolution. Wealthfront is looking into using AI to automate investment practices and provide customers with better and cheaper investments.

Next, social networking continues to be a vast AI playground. With facial recognition, geotagging, and chatbots, more and more people rely on social media platforms to get by. In the future, we expect chatbots to recommend shopping purchases, remind us of errands and tasks, and even meet people through AI chatbots via social networks.

On the other hand, homes are not spared from AI innovations. In fact, Mark Zuckerberg, Facebook's CEO, is working on a Jarvis replica. The goal is to come up with a superintelligence like in the movie Ironman, where devices in your home can communicate with each other, appliances turn on automatically depending on your needs, temperature adjusts, and turns on the TV to your favorite programs. With smart assistants such as Alexa and Echo devices, that vision looks very close.

Lastly, healthcare also shows some promising innovations. Robots may do risky surgeries such as brain and heart surgeries. Robots can be programmed according to precise accuracy and perform the surgery quickly. Minuscule robots can even explore the innermost parts of our bodies and send 3D images that will allow surgeons and health experts to determine symptoms and prevent sicknesses from becoming more serious.

# CONCLUSION

Now that you have learned about the wonderful AI innovations, and how it has made our lives better, you will surely appreciate the future more. People may think that making things more accessible is not the answer because it teaches people to become lazy. Personally, doing away with the mundane tasks and boring routine allows a person to have more time for creativity.

The promise of artificial intelligence also encourages creative minds to become more creative. When people exercise their minds, they become more intelligent. As you know, intelligence is hereditary, so we'll have more intelligent genes in the future.

Going back to artificial intelligence, as you have read from the previous chapter AI is not just about convenience and efficiency, it is all about saving lives. With many innovations that aim to preserve and save lives, people will be happier and develop better relationships and better communities.

Thank you again for buying this book!

I hope this book was able to help you to understand the amazing benefits of artificial intelligence, and how it has become an integral part of our lives.

Finally, if you enjoyed this book, then I'd like to ask you for a favor, would you be kind enough to leave a review for this book? It'd be greatly appreciated!

Thank you and good luck!